# IncogNegro

## Poetic Reflections on
## Race & Diversity in America

### HANNIBAL B. JOHNSON

PublishAmerica
Baltimore

First printing

PublishAmerica has allowed this work to remain exactly as the author intended, verbatim, without editorial input.

ISBN: 1-60474-696-3
PUBLISHED BY PUBLISHAMERICA, LLLP
www.publishamerica.com
Baltimore

Printed in the United States of America

# Acknowledgements

*Special thanks to those who offered feedback at various stages of the writing process, including: Cheryl Brown, Nancy Day, Andre 'Good, and Arlene Johnson. Thanks to Dr. Cornell Thomas for contributing a provocative foreword, and to Albert E. Dotson, Jr., Rabbi Charles P. Sherman, and Dr. Lonnie R. Williams for offering flattering jacket comments.*

# TABLE OF CONTENTS

# FOREWORD

Star Trek fans are familiar with the cloaking device. So are many others. The Klingons, once an archenemy of the Federation, cloaked their starships in order to gain a pre-attack strategic advantage over their enemies. However, in order to fire upon their adversaries, Klingons were required to uncloak—to become visible for all to see.

Over time, the Federation starships began to find ways to detect Klingon starships, even while they were cloaked. The Federation starships thus gained the power to see clearly the challenges before them. They were therefore able to take the actions necessary to meet those challenges head on.

Like the Klingons, we often cloak issues of inequality and discrimination by attributing differences between and among human beings to "the natural order of things." We internalize well-developed, socially constructed beliefs about our relative value. Some of us become invisible or subhuman in the eyes of others and, sadly, sometimes in our own eyes.

Rationalizing differences in this way provides the justification needed for some of us to treat others of us less favorably. It also cloaks the truth.

*IncogNegro* helps us uncloak the kind of thinking, believing, and actions that continue to divide us as a nation, especially along racial lines. These reflections on race and diversity in America will touch your heart, your very soul, and make you want to—no, **make you**—holler, "Stop the Madness!"

It is time to start a new, more positive chapter in our history. *IncogNegro* helps us to do just that.

    **– Dr. Cornell Thomas**, *Vice President, Institutional Diversity, Oklahoma State University*

# PROLOGUE

Racism is part of America's fabric and deeply woven into her history. Though no longer fashionable, racism remains for many an undergarment buried beneath layers and layers of bright, trendy clothing, unseen, but an essential part of the ensemble.

In a host of ways, from individual actions to institutional policies and practices, in matters of race we continue to don our historical hand-me-downs. Coming to terms with our racialized past through recognition, reparation, and reconciliation remains among our nation's unfinished business. Neglect, while it may sometimes forestall, generally exacerbates, and rarely cures. Our challenge: Mustering the courage in the present to examine, learn from, and act positively upon our past in the interest of our shared future.

My cohorts, the tail end of the baby boomers, constitute the integration generation, the first major wave of public school students to live out the United States Supreme Court's 1954 public school desegregation mandate. Many mid-twentieth century Americans, both "Negro" and white, idealized public school integration. For most, educational equity remained priority one. That said, integration, secondarily, held the allure of an enlightened pathway out of the abyss of racism. These devotees of transformational integration believed that as the "integration generation" matured into adulthood, gradual

9

change would occur throughout society. The positive lessons learned through trans-racial interaction would bleed into day-to-day living. Ossified attitudes would soften. A more open, egalitarian America would emerge.

In time, a harsh reality jolted the consciousness of these idealists. Significant segments of the white community vehemently opposed integration. Others only grudgingly acquiesced. Residential segregation, "creative" districting, "white flight," contemptible leadership, and a host of other factors kept many schools segregated. Pernicious institutional racism remained firmly ensconced.

We soon discovered that no court wielded power sufficient to banish racism. It took years for the states to carry out the United States Supreme Court mandate to end *de jure* segregation with all deliberate speed. *De facto* segregation persists even still.

Attitudes change glacially. Racism, which underlay forced separation of the races in the first instance, did not die when *de jure* segregation ended. Like the mythical Hydra, its other heads lurked ever so slightly beneath the surface. Race remains relevant.

Colored. Negro. Black. I moved through the public school system during the critical civil rights era. Though I never attended a segregated school, "integrated" does not fully define my public school experience. "Integration" implies a degree of unity, parity, and synergy that existed only on the margin.

Coming to terms with my blackness, my visible invisibility, required an examination of the watershed life experiences that colored my innocence with respect to matters of race. Moreover, it necessitated reflection on the broader, unifying concept of diversity—the many and varied ways in which we as individuals differ from one another. Understanding the social construct we call race and the moral imperative of diversity has been essential to my own identity awareness.

Valuing diversity—exercising diversity leadership—means treating others with respect and dignity, ferreting out injustice, celebrating differences, and simultaneously seeking common ground.

Acknowledge differences—celebrate them—but embrace the

fundamental sameness we share as human beings. Differences aside, we share basic values, goals, and aspirations. Most importantly, we share a common humanity. Tapping into that common humanity requires wading out of the shallow waters of difference as division and plunging headfirst into the deep pools of diversity as dynamism.

One of the ways that we may come to understand and appreciate diversity is to listen to the narratives others have to tell about their personal journeys, especially those related to differences, be they based on race, ethnicity, national origin, gender, religion, sexual orientation, or any of the other major identity markers. These tales shape our lives.

My stories of race and diversity, told poetically, follow. Listen.

Listening breeds empathy, evokes compassion, and moves us a step closer to walking the proverbial mile in someone else's shoes. Everything begins with that first step. Ultimately, like actors on the world stage, each of us has some role, however small, to play in fostering an accepting, inclusive, diverse community.

# I. BLACKNESS

# *As If*

As if shackles never bound.
As if lashes never welted.
As if rape never traumatized.
As if slip knots never hanged.
As if knives never pierced.
As if fire never charred.
As if bullets never silenced.

As if you see right past me.
As if I have no soul.
As if I too were not human.
As if my blackness should be cured.

As if freedom were free.
As if justice meant "just us."
As if separate were equal.
As if Jim never crowed.
As if we moved with all deliberate speed.
As if our rights came civilly.
As if our actions were affirmative.
As if our opportunities were equal.

As if time heals all wounds.
As if bygones could be bygones.
As if regret remedied.
As if acknowledgment atoned.
As if forgiveness were reflexive.
As if reconciliation came without sacrifice.

As if race no longer mattered.
As if meritocracy were universal.
As if privilege ceased to exist.
As if power were diffuse.

As if roots were extracted.
As if history no longer hobbled us.
As if psychic scars ever vanished.
As if we could start over.

As if words were solutions.
As if listening were hearing.
As if it were so simple.
As if we would just go along.
As if we could just get along.

As if you really know me.
As if you really care.
As if you see the future.
As if you see me there.
As if we share a destiny.

As if what is must be.
As if it were inevitable.
As if destiny were predetermined.
As if God were finished.

As if time stood still.
As if power came from without.
As if we were but pawns.
As if we should simply surrender.

As if we could all rise up.
As if we could wrest control.
As if we could all come together.
As if we could see the forest through its trees.

As if....
As if....
As if....
As if a change is gonna come.

## Minstrelsy Redux

We shuck and we jive,
We rant and we roar;
We call our selves bitches,
We call our selves whores.
Fed up with the madness,
Can't take it no more.

Style over substance,
Laughter masks pain;
The brags and the boasts
Shallow and vain.
Up from slavery,
Now enslaved again.

No need for blackface,
Already we're black;
Without even thinking,
Brought minstrelsy back.
Mindless. Senseless.
How'd we get on this track?

We degrade and debase,
We mock and we scorn,
Like minstrelsy before us,
Tired. Shop-worn.
We're gigglin' and grinnin'
While our forebears mourn.

The music, the venues,
They're modern and hip.
Entertain the masses.
Just lettin' 'er rip!
Makin' that money
On the minstrelsy tip.

We don't understand,
We don't seem to care,
How others perceive us,
The cross that we bear.
Trapped in the moment,
Entranced by each stare.

Jim Crow would be proud,
And ole Sambo, too,
Of how we've embraced them,
Birthed minstrelsy anew.
Don't seem to get it,
Don't know what to do.

Call me old fashioned,
Alarmist and shrill.
Call me a traitor,
Or better still....
Just stop the madness,
Forever and for real.

## To the N<sup>th</sup> Power
## The N Word Past & Present

Innocent roots.
The Latin *Niger*.
The French *Negre*.
Both basic black.

Twists and turns.
Chattel slavery.
White dominance,
Black subjugation.

The birth of
The N word,
A bastardization
Of basic black.

The N word.
A vile epithet.
A tool of white supremacy.

Demeaning.
Debasing.
Dehumanizing.

*Sui generis*: in a class by itself.

N-lover
N-ish
N-work
N-flicker
N-luck
N-lipping
N-knocker
N-rich
N-shooter
N-steak
N-stick
N-in the woodpile
N-creek
N-town

White-N
Yellow-N
Prairie-N
Sand-N

In the 1870s, a puzzle game called "Chopped Up Ns";
"N-Hair Smoking Tobacco."

A 1916 magazine advertisement
Depicts a black child
Drinking ink.
The caption: "N Milk."

Lazy
Dim-witted
Bug-eyed
Thick-lipped
Jet black
Immoral
Unkempt

Haggard
Infantile
Promiscuous
Parasitic

All stereotypical characteristics of the N.

The N word—
Offensive to the $N^{th}$ degree.

Some seek to turn this blunt instrument of oppression
Into something less sinister—
To co-opt the word;
To remove its taboo, and hence its sting.

The N word as a parallel
To Negro or black or African-American:
"What's going on, my N?"
The N word as a reference to vague, negative qualities:
"He's just a good-for-nothing N."
The N word as term of endearment:
"Those are my Ns!"

The N word—
No matter how hard we try
We cannot escape its history—
Its association
With racist caricatures,
With lynching,
With rape,
With whippings,
With pogroms,
With domestic terrorism,
With wholesale oppression.

It is impossible to fully understand that history
Without understanding something of the power of the N word.

Given that history,
Given all the alternatives:
"My Black Brother" or "My Black Sister";
"My Nubian King" or "My Nubian Queen"—
Why take the low road?

The N word:
Know the history.
Think before you speak.

## I Woke Up Black This Morning

I woke up black this morning.
Consciously black.
Aware that my blackness
Telegraphs a message to many
Before they even know my name.

I woke up black this morning.
Consciously black.
In a world color-struck;
In a self-deluding world—
In a world that believes itself
To be colorblind.

I woke up black this morning.
Consciously black.
Not troubled by my race-consciousness,
But by the racism that precipitated it.

I woke up black this morning.
Consciously black.
Knowing that my blackness may
Put me at considerable disadvantage
When I—

    Buy a house.
    Seek a bank loan.
    Purchase an automobile.
    Apply for a job.

Drive through a neighborhood.
Shop for merchandise.

I woke up black this morning.
Consciously black.
Ready to confront a demon
That is—

Institutional.
Pervasive.
Insidious.
Pernicious.
Chameleon-like.

I woke up black this morning.
Consciously black.
Not seduced by the myth of meritocracy.
Not persuaded by the propaganda of bootstraps.
Yet determined to fight on.

I woke up black this morning.
Consciously black.
Jaded by experience;
Scorched by past fires.
Bloodied, but unbowed.

I woke up black this morning.
Consciously black.
Looking toward the horizon,
Where equality looms like the sun.

I woke up black this morning.
Consciously black.
Planted in the present.
Aware of the past.
Focused on the future.

I woke up black this morning.
Consciously black.
With spirits high.
With hope intact.
Ready to take on the world.

*Till Death Do Us Part*

A teenage boy,
Just fourteen.
Northern exposure,
Southern roots.
Handsome.
Innocent.
Carefree.
Unknowing.
Unsuspecting.
Unaware.

Summer vacation.
Mississippi holiday.
1955.
Back down home.

A scorching summer sun.
A warm, gentle breeze.
Cousins and friends.
Southern hospitality.

In a country store,
One white-hot day,
The boy shows his boyness.
Pretty clerk catches his eye.
He lets loose a whistle,
Causes her to bristle.
No need to wonder why.

Black boy didn't know his place.
Southern customs.
White women and pedestals.
Mandingo myths.
Sexual attraction, real or imagined:
Racial taboos.

They hunted him down.
Beat and tortured and shot him.
Taught him a lesson.
Gin fan anchored to his body,
He sank to the bottom of the Tallahatchie.
Strange fruit he was,
Southern-style *fruit de Mer*.

A farce of a trial,
Two white men went free.
Murderers?
You can't commit murder without a human victim.
The black boy, at that time and in that place, wasn't human.

Sold their story to *Look*.
Now the nation knew.

Brave Mother Mamie forced us to see.
Open casket,
Photographers present.
Pictures in *Jet*.
Grotesque.
Bloated.
Monstrous.
Hideous.
Look what hate had wrought.

That boy, Emmett,
In plain view.
No longer handsome.
No longer innocent.
But somehow free.

That boy, Emmett,
Lives on in us.
Till death do us part.

## AUTHOR'S NOTE

In August 1955, a fourteen-year-old African-American boy went to visit relatives near Money, Mississippi. The boy, Emmett Till, knew about racism and segregation. He experienced segregation in his hometown of Chicago. Emmett, however, was unaccustomed to the extreme forms of racism that he encountered in Mississippi.

Emmett breached social mores by flirting with a white woman, Carolyn Bryant, in a local store. A few days later, two men barged into the cabin of Mose Wright, Emmett's uncle, in the middle of the night. Roy Bryant, the owner of the store and Carolyn's husband, and J.W. Milam, his brother-in-law, drove off with Emmett. Three days later, Emmett's lifeless, mutilated body turned up in the Tallahatchie River. Emmett's corpse was virtually unrecognizable. One of his eyes had been gouged out. His skull had been crushed. He had been shot.

Emmett's mother, Mamie, held an open casket funeral in Chicago. The gruesomeness of Emmett's remains shocked the conscience of many Americans.

An all-white jury acquitted Roy Bryant and J.W. Milam of Emmett's murder. They later confessed. The case galvanized the civil rights movement.

## Black Wall Street

Greenwood Avenue,
*a.k.a.* Black Wall Street,
In the Oil Capital of the World.

Entrepreneurs and innovators,
Black men; black women.
Bold.
Visionary.
Of national renown.

Doctors and lawyers,
Musicians and morticians,
Theaters, shine shops, and beauty parlors.

Greenwood—Black Wall Street—
Rife with activity and excitement.

Black gold lubricating the local economy,
Creating mostly white wealth,
But also trickling down—
Down Greenwood way.

Dollars circulating
Again and again and again.

An insular economy
Born of necessity
And sustained as a matter of pride.

Greenwood booming.
Greenwood bustling.
Greenwood beckoning.

Tulsa, Oklahoma,
The Magic City.
Oil barons.
Crude millionaires.

Not Deep South,
But Southern.

Black.
White.
Indian.
Diversity
In a sometimes combustible mix.

Boomtown.
Powder keg.

Black prosperity.
Demands for full citizenship.
Racial stereotypes.
Sexual taboos.

Jealousy.
Envy.
Racism.
The Ku Klux Klan.
A yellow journal.

A black shoeshine boy, Dick Rowland.
A white elevator girl, Sarah Page.
The downtown Drexel Building.

31

A mysterious ride.
The two emerge:
Sarah screaming;
Dick fleet of foot.

The *Tulsa Tribune*.
An inflammatory article:
*Nab Negro for Attacking Girl in an Elevator*.
A thinly veiled rape charge
That Sarah would ultimately recant.
An incitement to riot.

"There's gonna be a lynching!"
The talk of the town.
Dick Rowland: that boy is going down.

The arrest of Dick Rowland.
His confinement in jail.

Sheriff McCullough makes a solemn vow:
Dick Roland will be protected.

A burgeoning white mob.
Thousands milling,
Menacing the courthouse lawn.

Black men set out to protect Dick Rowland.
Marching.
Trudging toward the courthouse.

White and black meet.
An exchange of shouts and curses.
A struggle.
Shots ring out.

Roving gangs loot pawnshops.
They seize caches of weapons.

The armed mob spills out over the Frisco tracks
And fans deep into Greenwood.

Looting.
Shooting.
Burning.
Terrorizing.

Hunting savages in "Little Africa."
Wild Kingdom.

Local law enforcement deputizes mob members.
The mob prevents firemen from doing their job.

Minutes pass.
Hours pass.
Time moves ahead
Even as the clock of civilization turns decidedly backward.

Apocalypse now.
The National Guard intervenes.
Late.
Too late.
But better late than never.

Greenwood lay in ruin.
Black Wall Street crumbled.

Hundreds dead.
Thousands injured.
Black men in interment camps throughout the city.
Homeless everywhere.

The American Red Cross provides relief.
Tent cities emerge.
Life, for some, goes on.

No one in the white mob
Is ever held accountable.
No one.
Ever.

The city commission blamed the Negroes.
So did the grand jury.

They called it a "race riot."
It still stands as America's worst.

1921. May 31$^{st}$ and June 1$^{st}$ of 1921.
Not so long ago.

Greenwood rose from the ashes,
Despite the odds,
With little outside help,
Bigger, better, bolder.

Integration, urban renewal, the new economy:
Greenwood fell victim again.
And again she rose up.

Education, history, and culture.
The new Greenwood speaks to these.
Another incarnation;
Fresh promise and new possibilities.
The triumph of the human spirit.

## *I Don't Think of You As*

You're so professional.
I don't think of you as.

You're so articulate.
I don't think of you as.

You're so driven.
I don't think of you as.

You're so punctual.
I don't think of you as.

You're so well read.
I don't think of you as.

You're so cultured.
I don't think of you as.

You're so much like us.
I don't think of you as.

I don't think of you as.

I don't think of you as.

I don't think.

*Passing*

Skin the right shade,
Hair fine—no braid,
Undetectably black, I'm passing.

Speech quite refined,
Manner suitably sublime,
Undetectably black, I'm passing.

You cannot see,
The color in me,
Undetectably black, I'm passing.

Denying deep roots,
Enjoying white fruits,
Undetectably black, I'm passing.

Selling my soul,
Success is the goal,
Undetectably black, I'm passing.

Scaling the ladder,
Race is no matter,
Undetectably black, I'm passing.

Fly on the wall,
Hearing it all,
Undetectably black, I'm passing.

Should I reveal?
Someone might squeal,
Undetectably black, I'm passing.

Imitation of life,
Spare me this strife,
Undetectably black, I'm passing.

Now I know,
This charade must go,
Undetectably black, I'm passing.

Before my life's end,
I'll no longer pretend,
Undetectably black, I'm passing.

## Chocolate City (Vanilla Swirl)

Chocolate city, you say?
Just how chocolate?

Who's the producer?
Who's the produce?

Chocolate city, you say?
Just how chocolate?

Who scripts the action?
Who follows the script?

Chocolate city, you say?
Just how chocolate?

See who's on stage,
But know who's behind the curtain.

Chocolate city, you say?
Just how chocolate?

Who's the marionette?
Who's pulling the strings?

Chocolate city, you say?
Just how chocolate?

Sometimes appearances deceive
And numbers lie
And color fades.

Chocolate city, you say?
Chocolate...
But with a vanilla swirl.

## Dry Tears

I wept dry tears this morning,
Scanning the local news;
Another life destroyed,
Another lyric for my blues.

I wept dry tears this morning,
Last night's horrors came to light;
The victim died a senseless death,
Some black man lost his sight.

I wept dry tears this morning,
Lying there in bed;
Torn up by the violence,
Shattered by bloodshed.

I wept dry tears this morning,
For the killer and the killed;
For lives lost forever,
For voices ever stilled.

I wept dry tears this morning,
Thinking 'bout misspent youth;
Thinking 'bout what might have been,
Thinking 'bout ultimate truth.

I wept dry tears this morning,
For my brothers who've slipped so far;
Who so devalue human life,
Who lower for all the bar.

I wept dry tears this morning,
Wondering what went wrong,
Wondering how to fix it,
Wondering, Lord, how long?

I wept dry tears this morning,
Knowing I alone can't solve;
This looming American crisis,
Together we must resolve.

I wept dry tears this morning,
No moisture left in me;
No outward signs of despair,
Nothing one could see.

I wept dry tears this morning,
Not knowing what to do;
Not knowing how to make it right,
Without, it seems, a clue.

I wept dry tears this morning,
No more, not again;
Determined to make a difference,
In the lives of these lost men.

# The Race Card

You say I played the race card.
I say I played what's dealt.
You say there was no basis,
I say it's what I felt.

You say other issues,
Explain it, truth be told.
I say it's the system,
If I may be so bold.

You say it's so tired,
So bland, so blah—cliché,
I say that's the real world,
That race is here to stay.

You say you're blind to color,
That race you do not see.
I say that's impossible,
Race will always be.

You say just keep quiet,
Ignore race and go on.
I say, "How insightful!
Poof—now race be gone!"

You say things are better,
Laws have now been passed.
I say look beyond that,
See the die as cast.

You say I don't get it,
Don't want to let it go.
I say I'm frustrated,
With progress all too slow.

You say I'm self-righteous,
Mired in my own doubt.
I say I'm reflecting,
What I know about.

You say let's just end this,
Let's dwell on this no more.
I say that's the problem,
Closing yet another door.

# The Lynching of Mary Turner

Mary Turner spoke up one day.
Stood up and said her piece
Knowing not what else to do,
She begged for Hayes' release.

Mary Turner spoke up one day,
Said, "Dear God, this isn't fair."
Hanging Hayes, my husband,
No conscience, without a care.

Mary Turner spoke up one day,
Voice raised for one last time.
Said justice and morality,
Made lynching Hayes a crime.

Mary Turner spoke up one day,
Not knowing what she'd wrought.
What evil lurked within their hearts,
What hell to then be caught.

Mary Turner spoke up one day,
They knocked her to her knees.
Silenced her for good, they did,
Swung her in the breeze.

Mary Turner spoke up one day,
They set her body alight.
Baby ripped right from her womb,
A savage, ghastly sight.

Mary Turner spoke up one day,
Appealed for justice and peace.
With Mary and her unborn child,
The violence would not cease.

Mary Turner spoke up one day,
Spoke out for you and me.
Upon her shoulders we still stand,
Martyred so we'd be free.

## AUTHOR'S NOTE

In May of 1918, a white plantation owner in Brooks County, Georgia, got into a quarrel with one of his African-American tenants. The tenant killed him. A white mob sought to avenge the plantation owner's death. Unable to locate the suspect, the mob instead seized upon and lynched an innocent man, Hayes Turner.

Turner's wife, Mary, at the time eight months pregnant, incensed the mob when she threatened to have its members arrested for Hayes' murder. The next morning, several hundred white men took Mary Turner from her home to a local stream. They tied her ankles together and hung her head downward from a tree. After dousing her clothes with gasoline, they set her alight. One man split Mary's abdomen open with a knife. An unborn child fell from her womb. A man crushed the child's head under his heel. The mob riddled Mary Turner's maimed body with bullets.

## Raising the Race
### The Great Washington-Du Bois Debate Redux

Self-help.
Racial solidarity.
Accommodation.

The crafts.
Industry.
Farming.

Patience.
Enterprise.
Thrift.

Earn white acceptance
And gradual integration.

Educator.
Reformer.
Statesman.

**Booker T. Washington.**

Higher education.
Political action.
Civil rights.

The Talented Tenth.

Thought shepherds.
Cultural missionaries.

Leadership.
Agitation.
Protest.

Demand a seat at the political table
And full civic participation.

Intellectual.
Scholar.
Political strategist.

*W.E.B. Du Bois.*

Two men
Who both wanted
The best of us
From the rest of us.

Two men
Who believed in the promise
Of America.

They believed in life.
They believed in liberty.
They believed in the pursuit of happiness.

They believed in an America in which they did not live.
They believed in an America in which they did not die.
Yet, they both, at least for a time, believed.

The great African-American debate of the early twentieth century
Rages still in the twenty-first.

The culture of poverty.
Impoverished for lack of
Education, ambition, and values?
Or impoverished on account of systemic racism
And political powerlessness?

Self-help versus governmental intervention.
Economic self-sufficiency versus the welfare state.
Business development versus political prowess.

Cast down your buckets
Where you are.
Pull firmly on your bootstraps.
Take responsibility for your own destiny.
Show them your mettle.
In time, equality in all things social will come.

Lift every voice
In political protest against injustice.
Petition for redress of grievances.
Demand quality education.
Make them respect you.
Wait no more: Now is the time.

Either or.
N'er the twain shall meet.

An ideological chasm too deep to span
Or an artful—but false—dichotomy?

Must truth reside so absolutely in these absolutes?
Might not we find wisdom on both shores?

The dust from the fracas
Obscures our common ground.

Taking advantage of the opportunities that abound.
Doing our part to ensure that those opportunities are equally distributed.
Working to spread the word—to communicate opportunities as they
    arise.

Educating ourselves.
Supporting our families.
Leading in our communities.
Fostering governmental accountability—
Making sure that our representatives
Represent us, too.

Envisioning a future
That honors the past,
Takes into account the present,
And stretches us to the outer reaches of our potential.

On these, can we not agree?

And on belief in self.
And on personal empowerment.
And on the power of hope.

Neither conservative nor liberal,
Neither Washington nor Du Bois.
Somewhere on terra firma in between.

## Black Fugue

Voices.
Swirling in my head.
Angry voices.
Combatants.
Hopeful voices.
Peacemakers.
Voices dancing.
Vying over which will lead
And which will follow.
Ebbing.
Flowing.
Tides of supremacy.
Waves of subservience.

Voices.
Swirling in my head.
Melodious voices.
Discordant voices.
Contrapuntal voices.

Black fugue.
Soothing and shattering.
Comforting and confining.
Freezing and freeing.

Voices.
Swirling in my head.
Past voices—voices of what was.

Future voices—voices of what might be.
My own voice goes missing.

Voices.
Swirling in my head.

Is it normal?
Am I sane?

Black fugue.
Abnormal normality.
Insane sanity.

Black.

Fugue.

## Shades of Black

As a caramel colored brother I fail to see,
The fundamental difference between you and me.
Despite clear variations in pigment and tint,
A little dab 'il do ya—black 100%.
We come in shades of black, in various hues—
    Caramel colored
    *Café au lait*
    Butter pecan
    Mellow yellow
    Jet black
    Sepia toned
    Red bone
    Peanut brittle
    Dark chocolate
    Milk chocolate
    Mahogany
    High yellow
    Blue black
Just to name a few.
We come in shades of black, in various hues,
That's the story, now here's the news.
As a caramel colored brother I fail to see,
The fundamental difference between you and me.
Despite clear variations in pigment and tint,
A little dab 'il do ya—black 100%.

## *Angry Black Man*

Yeah, I'm angry.
You'd be angry, too…

   If jails and prisons housed a quarter of your brothers.
   If the scourge of AIDS ravaged your 'hood.
   If drugs and drug dealers ruled your world.
   If showing your true colors referred to gang affiliation, not
      character.
   If your schools produced not-ready-for-prime-time players.
   If you were statistically as likely to be in prison as in college.
   If your color affected the quality of your health care.
   If your pigment impacted your prospects for employment.
   If the word "profile" meant something police do, not a photographic
      angle.
   If American history Xed you out: ignored, marginalized, or
      misrepresented you.
   If, despite analysis, assessment, and diagnosis, "the system" that
      oppresses you never got fixed.

Yeah, I'm angry.
You'd be angry, too.

## Dirty Laundry

We don't air our dirty laundry.
See, it's about family.
We take care of our own.
One way or the other.
Internally.

We stick up for those who stand up.
Our leaders get much respect, troubled times notwithstanding.

Crack smokers.
Philanderers.
Kickback kings.
One and all,
Personal peccadilloes
And major character flaws
Aside.

We're parties to a non-aggression pact.
We figure The Man already takes his aggression out on us.
We need to give a brother a break, feel me?

It's not about the crackhead
Or the philanderer
Or the brother on the take.

It's about the system,
The set-up,
The Man who's pulling the strings.

We chose our leaders.
We hire.
We fire.
We take care of our own.

In our own way.
In our own time.

We rally 'round when you attack one of ours.

It's a black thing.
It's about survival.
(And we know something about survival.)

You can't hamper us
With our own dirty laundry.

## *Bitter Roots*

He grew more bitter,
Year upon year;
Exacting his vengeance,
As the end drew near.

His life flashed before him,
So vivid and true;
Things long forgotten,
Emerged from the blue.

He recalled the darkness,
Of days gone by.
He relived the horrors,
Born of one big lie.

The slights, the stares
The brutality, too;
The black man's burden,
The days he did rue.

He hated all white men,
For what some had done.
He refused to consider,
That they are not one.

The bitterness that killed him,
Helped not his cause.
It kept him from living,
Gave racism no pause.

## Homeland Insecurity

1919 in America.

World War I: ended.

Black soldiers returned from the European theater.
Returned from fighting for the homeland:
For America.
For freedom.
For justice.
For equality.
For the American way.

For the American way:
White hegemony.
White supremacy.
White dominance.

Returned to an America
Du Bois described.
An America at war with her own ideals.
An American losing the battle.

An America that lynched us.
An America that disenfranchised us.
An America that stole from us: our land, our labor, our opportunity.
An America that insulted, degraded, and debased us.
A fundamentally un-American America.

A loathing America.
*A laissez-faire* America (at least as it pertained to Negroes).
A lethal America.

Marginalized.
Mocked.
Murdered.

Homeland insecurity.
Predictable unpredictability.

Returned as foreign natives;
Visiting residents.

Returned to "race riots"
And to lynchings
For which we, of course,
Were to blame.

To joblessness
And poverty
And utter despair.

To a two-faced Uncle Sam:
Avuncular in wartime,
Abusive during the peace.

To the American melting pot
Only to discover
Ourselves missing
From the ingredient list.

Time passed.
Little changed.

World War II.

Time passed.
Little changed.

Korea.

Time passed.
Little changed.

Vietnam.

Time passed.
Things began to change.

The 1960's Civil Rights Movement.

Progress at home.
A more American America.

Ideals not fully realized,
But hope on the horizon.

Operation Desert Shield.
Operation Desert Storm.
Operation Enduring Freedom.
Operation Iraqi Freedom.

War abroad,
Skirmishes at home.

Now our soldiers return.
Return from fighting.
Return to a homeland more secure.

# The Ghetto Way

Can't seem to getaway
From the ghetto way.
Can't seem to getaway
From the ghetto way.
Can't lose my strut,
Can't hide my swagger.
Even my blood pulses
To a syncopated hip-hop beat.

Can't seem to getaway
From the ghetto way.
Tight braids, low fades,
A thousand different looks.
My mind races,
Imagining what's missed and missing.

Can't seem to getaway
From the ghetto way.
Dealers and hustlers,
Schemes and scams.
But mostly ordinary people,
Just makin' it.

Can't seem to getaway
From the ghetto way.
School of hard knocks,
Proving ground.
If I can make it there,
Well, I can....

Can't seem to getaway
From the ghetto way.
Part of me,
Inside my head.
No turning back,
Embedded in the spirit.

Can't seem to getaway
From the ghetto way.

## Black Enough

My clothing: modest,
No sagging to the knee.
Am I black enough?
Well, black enough for me.

My English: standard,
Proper to a tee.
Am I black enough?
Well, black enough for me.

My friends: eclectic,
My choices, free.
Am I black enough?
Well, black enough for me.

My thirst: knowledge,
As deep as the sea.
Am I black enough?
Well, black enough for me.

My focus: forward,
To be all I can be.
Am I black enough?
Well, black enough for me.

My message: unity,
Acceptance is key.
Am I black enough?
Well, black enough for me.

My allegiance: questioned,
By those who cannot see.
That I'm black enough:
Black enough for me.

## Pops

Inching up imperceptibly on him,
In all manner of ways,
Under cover of darkness,
In the afternoon haze.

Creases on his smoothness,
Missteps in his stride,
A thousand little differences,
Imperfections he can't hide.

Lack luster where the shine was,
Distortion in the clear,
These minor deteriorations,
Growing major year by year.

A voice that once did bellow,
Now barely I can hear,
A man who once seemed fearless,
Seems sheepish when I'm near.

A fierce and dogged intellect,
That once did challenge all,
Hides beneath a frail veneer,
Unresponsive to my call.

Less bitter than he once was,
Less given to a fight,
Black warrior in the struggle,
Now slipping into night.

Time's a mighty leveler,
As we age our way along,
Our bodies always fail us,
Ending life's sweet song.

## Messiah Days

Those people.
There.
Them.

What are they thinking?
What do they want?
Who speaks for them?
Who's their leader?

They need a Douglass
Or a Du Bois;
A Washington;
A Randolph;
Another King;
Perhaps even an "X."

They need a guide.
They need a spokesperson.
They need a thought leader.
They need an icon.
They need a savior—a messiah.

Lord, what became of those messiah days?

What to do, no messiah ascending?

What if we each rose up?
What if we all stood strong?
What if our many voices spoke truth to power?
What if each of us tapped into the messiah within?

Messiah days no more.

## Self-Help

You people.
You need to take responsibility.
You need to do for yourselves.
Stop looking to the government for breaks and handouts!

You people?
Responsibility?
*Take care* of us?

Who knows more about self-help than African-Americans?

Surviving slavery.
Outlasting lynching.
Jettisoning Jim Crow.

We live a history of official hostility.
We live a legacy of self-help.

Overcoming odds.
Swimming upstream.
Battling from the outside in.

We know something about self-help.
We could teach you a thing or two.

Step right on up.

It's self-serve.
Help yourself.

# II. Otherness

## IncogNegro

No Superman-like flight.
No Spiderman-like agility.
No x-ray vision.
No superhuman strength.
Just people power.
The power of observation.
The ability to listen—
At the most inopportune times
According to some.

He moves about freely
From his black world
Into the white world,
And all points in between.
Unimagined.
Unobtrusive.
Undetected.

IncogNegro.
Undercover brother.
The new black superhero.

He's the proverbial fly on the wall.
IncogNegro hears what's said
In the color vacuum.
When "they" aren't around.

The whispers.
The slurs.
The pandering.
The patronization.

In backrooms.
In boardrooms.
In country clubs.
In suites.
In the cozy comfort of sameness.

IncogNegro omniscient.

There's talk of the black problem—
Of welfare.
Of too many babies.
Of crime.
Of hypersexuality.
Of unnatural athleticism.
Of leaderlessness.
Of cultural decadence.
Of natural selection.
Of manifest destiny.
Of possible retribution
For wrongs not righted.

They speak to themselves,
For themselves.

They quake at the thought of discovery.
They maintain the public pretense—
Plentitude.
Equal opportunity.
Egalitarianism.
Secrets and lies.

The rich and the famous.
The powerful and the pious.
The political and the academic.
The white everyperson,
Though not *every* white person.

The exposure of their innermost thoughts
About the "other"—
Befuddlement.
Tolerance.
Indifference.
Guilt.
Hostility.
A risk too great to bear.

Social dialogue continues.
Magnanimous pronouncements abound.
Yet privately,
True selves emerge.
And nothing really changes.

IncogNegro, if ever revealed,
Must die.
He knows too much.
Knowledge is power.
And power is deadly.

Easier to kill IncogNegro
Or the hypocrisy upon which he feeds?

## *Those People*

"Those people," they're savages,
Not of our kin.
Their behavior—abhorrent,
Inhuman some contend.

"Those people," they're uncivilized,
Uncouth and unclean.
They're beastly—animalistic,
Let's say what we mean.

"Those people," they're aliens,
Foreigners and more.
They're threatening—outsiders,
Crossing borders and shores.

"Those people," they're immoral,
Debauched and debased.
They're scurrilous—scandalous,
Mere human waste.

"Those people," they're ignorant,
Content to be less.
They're incorrigible—corrupted,
Sad to confess.

"Those people," they're criminals,
They lie and they steal,
They're vicious—vile,
A plague all too real.

"Those people," they're among us,
Without and within.
They are us—humanity,
Though otherwise we pretend.

## *White Privilege*

Unearned and unspoken,
Invisible to the eye,
This bundle of benefits,
We cannot deny.

This package of privilege,
Comes freely to me,
On account of my whiteness,
The first thing you see.

An amazing windfall,
By accident of birth,
Decisions triggered
About relative worth.

Perhaps if I give you,
An example, maybe two,
To illustrate the quandary,
You'd see things like I do.

When I speak out in public,
When I make my case,
There's no attribution,
To others of my race.

In most situations,
At least if I so choose,
I'll be the majority,
Less likely to lose.

Less likely to be followed,
Less likely to be stopped,
Less likely to be mistreated,
Less likely to be dropped.

I didn't choose my color,
Nor unearned benefit.
I am not responsible,
Just taking what I can get.

## Red Summer

Streets of crimson.
Bad blood.
Blood lust.
Blood sport.
Bloodthirsty mobs.
Hunting season.
Black game.

Ruptured cities.
Hemorrhagic violence.
In cold blood.

Chicago, Illinois.
Omaha, Nebraska.
Washington, D.C.
Elaine, Arkansas.
Charleston, South Carolina.
Knoxville, Tennessee.
Longview, Texas.

Summer.
1919.
Red Summer, according to James Weldon Johnson.

"Race riots" in cities North and South.
Assaults on black communities.
Here, there, and everywhere.

Conflagration.
Race war.
Pogrom.
Holocaust.
Genocide.

Death.
Destruction.
Despair.

Claude McKay got it right.
If we must die,
Die nobly.
Die honorably.
If we must die,
Die fighting.

## One Hundred White Men

I do solemnly swear that I will support and defend the Constitution of the United States against all enemies, foreign and domestic; that I will bear true faith and allegiance to the same; that I take this obligation freely, without any mental reservation or purpose of evasion; and that I will well and faithfully discharge the duties of the office on which I am about to enter: So help me God.

Black men, women, and children brutalized
At the hands of white vigilantes
In front of leering white mobs.

Hung from trees.
Riddled with bullets.
Bludgeoned.
Pistol-whipped.
Charred beyond recognition.

Gruesome deaths.
Festive occasions.

Scores recorded each year.
Scores more went unrecorded.
Death.
Without dignity.

Wanton violence.
Callous brutality.
Inhuman cruelty.

80

A message to all Negroes.
A message about domination.
A message about subjugation.
A message about white supremacy.

One Hundred White Men.
A promise to uphold the Constitution.
And a deadly breach.

The United States House of Representatives passed anti-lynching
    legislation.

Once.
Twice.
Thrice.

The United States Senate rejected it.

Once.
Twice.
Thrice.

Even United States Presidents lobbied for the legislation.
To no avail.

Human rights abroad.
Racial wrongs at home.

One Hundred White Men.

Rhetoric.
Rationalizations.
Racism.

One Hundred White Men.
It's a question of states' rights.
Lynching keeps black brutes away from our white women.
Sometimes those Nigras need to be taught a lesson.
Keep 'em in their place.

One Hundred White Men.
Among them, Richard B. Russell Jr.,
Whom we honor with a United States Senate building.

Once.
Twice.
Thrice.

1922.
1937.
1940.

Finally, an apology
For the derelictions of One Hundred White Men.

A Senate Resolution.
Number 39.

This time, no debate.
This time, no filibuster.
This time, no blockage.

A voice vote.
No roll call.
Mississippi missing in action.

Survivors watching.
Descendants watching.
The world watching.

A victory.
Of sorts.

An apology.
An atonement.

A first.
At last.

100+ years—and 4,700+ lives—too late.

God help us.

## Black Rats

Black.
Male.
And suffering from syphilis.

Poor.
Illiterate.
Alabama sharecroppers.

Naïve.
Trusting.
Vulnerable.

Forty years.
1932 – 1972.
One experiment.

The Tuskegee Syphilis Experiment.

The United States Public Health Service,
Under the guise of treatment,
Turned these men into lab rats
For its own dubious, racist ends.

Black.
Male.
Lab rats.
399 of them.

"Bad blood."
The men were told
That they were being treated for
"Bad blood."

They were not being treated at all.
Autopsy data, not cures,
Motivated the Public Health Service.
Death.

Tumors.
Heart disease.
Paralysis.
Blindness.
Insanity.
Such are the ravages
Of untreated syphilis.
Then death.

No full disclosure.
No informed consent.
Lies.
Placebos.
And more lies.

Disease.
Death.
And diabolical doctors.

Free health care.
Phony drugs.
Feigning physicians.

Brought to media attention,
No longer shrouded in secrecy,
The experiment ended in 1972.

28 dead of syphilis.
100 dead of related complications.
40 wives infected with syphilis.
19 children born with congenital syphilis.
All in the name of science.

Human beings.
Black men.
Dehumanized.
Emasculated.

A racist Public Heath Service.
Black minions and collaborators, too.
Merchants of misery.
Masters of death.
All in the name of science.

Black
Lab
Rats.

We weep for them.
We weep for those who exploited them in the name of science.
We weep for a society that allowed the Tuskegee Syphilis Experiment
    to happen.


*The United States government did something that was wrong—
deeply, profoundly, morally wrong. It was an outrage to our
commitment to integrity and equality for all our citizens...clearly
racist.*
    **– President Bill Clinton**

*Apology for the Tuskegee Syphilis Experiment to eight survivors
(May 16, 1997)*

## The Bequest

Self-love.
Self-esteem.
Self-respect.
Pride.
Dignity.

Stake your claim.
They are our legacy,
Bequeathed by
Forefathers and foremothers
Whom we know
Only through the annals
Of an oft-forgotten history.

They came before the Mayflower,
Our ancestors,
Shackled cargo
Bound for foreign shores.
Welcome as chattel,
Unwelcome as human beings.

They came before the Mayflower,
Our ancestors,
A great middle passage
Africa-Atlantic-America.

Sowed the seeds of a great economic power,
Nurtured the scions of the ruling elite,
Worked fields,
Felled forests,
Built cities,
Raised monuments,
And fashioned music from misery.

All the while,
They suffered the indignities of color and caste.
Unable, temporarily,
To wrest loose the yoke of oppression.

So many served
Without being servile;
Played the fool
Without being foolish;
Feigned lack of knowledge
Without being ignorant.

Manumission.
Still more misery,
Still more suffering.
Still no surrender.

More work from within.

Self-love.
Self-esteem.
Self-respect.
Pride.
Dignity.

These things,
Coupled with hope,
Saw them through.

The cinch of the noose,
The heat of the fire,
The crack of the whip,
The thud of the truncheon,
The sting of the bullet,
The thrust of the knife,
The trauma of personal violation,
And all manner of depredations, degradations, and indignities.

None of these shook the core foundation
Of belief in self.

That is our gift.
Ours to carry forward.

Kings and queens.
That is our legacy.

We must believe ourselves to be kings and queens.
And we must acquit ourselves accordingly.

Self-love.
Self-esteem.
Self-respect.
Pride.
Dignity.

Stake your claim.
They are our legacy,
Bequeathed by
Forefathers and foremothers
Whom we know
Only through the annals
Of an oft-forgotten history.

Without them there is no future.
Without them there is no hope.

*Those Other All-American Looks*

All-American looks.
Mom, American.
Apple pie, American.
The flag, American.
All-American looks.

All-American looks.
Tanned.
Blond.
Blue-eyed.
All-American looks.

But what of those other Americans?
What of those other all-American looks?

Those other all-American looks.
Not "tanned."
Not blond.
Not blue-eyed.
Those other All-American looks.

Those other all-American looks.
Dark-skinned—naturally.
Dark-haired.
Dark-eyed.
Those other All-American looks.

Those other all-American looks.
Black.
Or brown.
Or red.
Perhaps yellow.
Those other all-American looks.

Those other all-American looks.
Many.
Varied.
Diverse.
Those other all-American looks.

Those other all-American looks.
Just remember the beauty
To be found in
Those other All-American looks.

## Helmsian Hype

"He *needed* that job," the voiceover announced as the working class, plaid-clad young white man strode languidly across the screen. "But they *gave* it to a minority," voice in appropriate diminuendo, air thick with resignation.

"He"?
White men writ large.

"Needed"?
Deserved.
Entitled.

"They"?
Government.
That bloated, unwieldy beast.

"Gave"?
Undeserving.
Unworthy.
Unearned.
Unqualified.
Affirmative Action.

"Minority"?
Black.

What a topsy-turvy world, that TV land!
Reality belies this Helmsian lore,

But drama trumps documentary every time.
Investigate.
Cogitate.
Participate.

See through the Helmsian Hype.

## AUTHOR'S NOTE

Jesse Alexander Helms, Jr., born October 18, 1921, is a former five-term Republican U.S. Senator from North Carolina, and a former chairman of the Senate Foreign Relations Committee. He was considered one of the leading figures of the modern "Christian right." In both 1990 and 1996, Helms won against Harvey Gantt, the former African-American mayor of Charlotte. Helms' 1990 victory was partially credited to a late-running television commercial that urged white voters to reject Gantt because of the Democratic candidate's support for affirmative action programs. The ad showed a white man's hands ripping up a rejection notice from a company that had not hired him on account of affirmative action policies that had *given* the job to a black person.

*Blood Borne*


Craniofacial phenotype—
Broad noses; thick lips; rounded features.
Skin color—
Dark (or at least relatively so).
Hair texture—
Thick; coarse; kinky; nappy.

Defining elements of blackness;
Elements of otherness.
Traits strong enough to warrant
Protection of the blood supply.

Blackness as contaminant.
Blackness as noxious.
Blackness as lethal.
Blackness without beauty.

Blood borne rules
For determining blackness
By process of elimination—
By contraposition—
And ensuring the purity
And the superiority
And the hegemony
Of those deemed
Non-black—
Of those with keener noses
And whiter skin

And lighter, straighter hair
And paler eyes
And more angular features.
The Eurocentric ideal
Foisted upon every continent.

Hypodescent.
The "one drop rule"
Imposed upon us
By social and political forces
Set in motion by ruling elites.
All in the blood.
Blackness as blood borne.

Blackness as liability.

Our blood.
Our sweat.
Our tears.

In trickles.
In tides.
In torrents.

The sacrifice.
The strife.
The struggle.

We embraced the blackness.
Co-opted hypodescent.
Savored the one drop.
Defined black from within.
Black became political—
A statement about
History

And caste
And class
And oppression
And uplift
And pride
And so much more.

Blackness as blood borne.
The Dark Continent.
Cradle of civilization.
The Mother Land.
Africa.
Ultimate genetic trading post.
Seminal DNA marketplace.
Where it all started.
From whence we all come.

Origin of the species.
Then migration.
Then evolution.
Then adaptation.

The one.
The few.
The many.

Black blood runs
Through all our veins.

And yet we still behave
As though we shared no past,
Had no common ancestors,
And might ultimately escape
Our conjoined destiny.

Blackness as blood borne.
We are all blood brothers and sisters;
All to some extent, then, black.

Check your bloodlines.

## Salad Days

Make mine a salad bowl.
For me, no melting pot.
Don't pretend you're colorblind.
Don't cast all as one big lot.

That melting pot folks speak of,
Metaphorically now and then,
Simplifies the real truth,
Denies where we've really been.

My people never melted,
Though seared by fire's heat,
Clinging to their essence,
Survival itself a feat.

Let's all tell our stories,
Let's relish who we are,
*Reductio ad absurdum*,
Sameness goes only so far.

Allow me to be different.
Respect me all the same.
Find what we share in common.
Know we're both in the game.

Like ingredients tossed in salad,
Each maintaining its own zest.
The color and flavor of differences,
Dress life's salad at its best.

Make mine a salad bowl.
For me, no melting pot.
Don't pretend you're colorblind.
Don't cast all as one big lot.

## *Our True Enemies*

Our true enemies,
Ignorance and fear,
Seem to expand,
Year after year.

At home and abroad,
Within and without,
Not knowing or caring,
Not feeling about.

Fearing this, fearing that,
All around the world,
Different tongues, different shades,
A different flag unfurled.

Not knowing the other,
Spells danger, you see,
Lest we know the other,
We'll never be free.

Fearing the other,
Holds similar fate,
Suspicions, mistrust,
Inability to relate.

Ignorance plus fear,
The formula for hate,
Interrupt the cycle,
Before it's too late.

Our true enemies,
Ignorance and fear,
Seem to expand,
Year after year.

## Walk a Mile in My Shoes

Walk a mile in my shoes.
Get to know and understand me.

See the sights that I see.
Hear the sounds that I hear.
Smell the aromas that I smell.
Taste the life that I taste.
Touch the things that I touch.

Take affirmative action.
Become the "O" amidst a sea of "Xs"—
The minority in the fishbowl,
Under the microscope,
In the glare of the spotlight.

How do you feel?
Lonely?
Isolated?
Patronized?
Pitied?
Unappreciated?
Alienated?
Estranged?
Unmoored?
Unloved?
Abandoned?
Alone?

Walk a mile in my shoes.
Get to know and understand me.

Trudge through my day-to-day realities.
Dance around being the target of suspicion
And the object of fear.
Leap into the realm of the highly visible invisible;
The existent nonexistent.
Skip over the abrading effects of underestimation and under-
    appreciation.
Run.

Walk a mile in my shoes.
Get to know and understand me.

My everyday experiences make me who I am.
They color my perspective.
They influence my thoughts.
They shape my dreams.

Why should you bother to know me?
Morality: It's the right thing to do.

Why should you bother to know me?
Self-interest: I'm worth it.

Why should you bother to know me?
Because I am.

To deny me is to deny your own humanity.

Walk a mile in my shoes.
Get to know and understand me.

Appreciate, don't denigrate.
Recognize, don't patronize.
Empathize, don't sympathize.

Learn from me.
Teach me.

We will grow together.

# III. ONENESS

## The Iceberg

I'm like a giant iceberg,
I'm more than what you see;
Really get to know me,
Imagine what might be.

Don't think that I'm not human,
No, I'm really just like you;
But I'm also like an iceberg,
'Til you know me through and through.

My eyes, my nose, my lips, my hair,
See them as I do;
They are not the answer,
They won't tell you who.

I may not talk like you do,
I may speak a different way;
But listen for the meaning,
In all of what I say.

My clothes might seem funny,
Not the latest style;
But it's the inside not the outside,
That matters all the while.

I may be red or yellow,
I may be black or white;
Look beyond my color,
Whether dark or light.

I may be rich, I may be poor,
I may not fit right in;
It's not about the money,
It's the person who's within.

Really get to know me,
My beauty you will see;
Get to know the real me,
That's the only way to be.

You may think you know me,
You might even fence me in;
But before you put me in that box,
Find out where I've been.

I may be who you think I am,
I may be more or less;
But you won't know, you never will,
Until you see my best.

You may think I'm funny,
You may even fear;
But don't be quick to judge me,
Just draw me ever near.

Though we may be different,
In a way or two;
We share much in common,
In what we see and do.

Treat me like I'm family,
Show me some respect;
We'll get along much better,
Each other we'll protect.

When we come together,
Out of many one;
To focus on our future,
Our journey yet begun.

Together we have power,
Divided we have none;
Let's decide, let's take a stand,
You and me as one.

I'm like a giant iceberg,
I'm more than what you see;
Really get to know me,
Imagine what might be.

## Integration Central

"Two, four, six, eight, we ain't gonna integrate!"

Heads cocked back.
Eyes piercing; darting.
Lips tightly pursed.
Bodies gyrating.
Arms flailing.

"Two, four, six, eight, we ain't gonna integrate!"

Children.
White children.
Teenagers.
Hundreds.
Hate-filled.
Beastly.
On the prowl.
Ready to pounce.

"Two, four, six, eight, we ain't gonna integrate!"

Heads held high.
Eyes fixed forward.
Lips slightly parted.
Bodies erect.
Arms by sides.

"Two, four, six, eight, we ain't gonna integrate!"

Children.
Black children.
Teenagers.
Nine.
Determined.
Defiant.
On a mission.
Ready to roll.

"Two, four, six, eight, we ain't gonna integrate!"

September 1957.
Little Rock, Arkansas.
Central High School.
Cacophonous.
Chaotic.
Calamitous.

"Two, four, six, eight, we ain't gonna integrate!"

An opportunistic politician.
An anti-integration platform.
A Governor named Faubus.
A "lily white" vow.
A school board resigned to integrate.
A collision course.

"Two, four, six, eight, we ain't gonna integrate!"


A compliant Arkansas National Guard.
A Governor's orders.
A crisis in the making.

"Two, four, six, eight, we ain't gonna integrate!"

A Mayor; a Mann.
A telegram to Washington.
A federalist President called Ike.
A request for federal troops.
An affirmative response.
A mandate to integrate.

"Two, four, six, eight, we ain't gonna integrate!"

The 101st Airborne Division.
1,000 men strong.
A descent into Little Rock.
The Little Rock Nine.
A 101st bodyguard for each.
An intervention.

"Two, four, six, eight, we ain't gonna integrate!"

A federalized Arkansas National Guard.
The United States supreme.
A *coup de gras.*

"Two, four, six, eight, we ain't gonna integrate!"

Attitudes hardened.
Bitterness took hold.
Anger persisted.

"Two, four, six, eight, we ain't gonna integrate!"

Spat upon.
Tripped up.
Insulted.

Beaten.
Doused with acid.
Their lockers vandalized.
One of their number expelled.

"Two, four, six, eight, we ain't gonna integrate!"

The closure of schools.
The interruption of lives.
A Governor's final gambit.

"Two, four, six, eight, we ain't gonna integrate!"

They endured.
Their innocence did not.

"Two, four, six, eight, we ain't gonna integrate!"

Integration Central.
With all deliberate speed.

*One Day in June*
*Juneteenth: An American Freedom Day*

Free at last.
Free at last.
Thank God Almighty,
We're free at last.

"[O]n the first day of January, in the year of our Lord one thousand
eight hundred and sixty-three, all persons held as slaves within any
State or designated part of a State, the people whereof shall then be
in rebellion against the United States, shall be then, thenceforward,
and forever free...."

Abraham Lincoln, *President of the United States of America*

Free at last.
Free at last.
Thank God Almighty,
We're free at last.

An all-American blood bath raged.
More than two years of internecine civil war.
Union versus Confederacy.
North versus South.
Brother pitted against brother.

Free at last.
Free at last.
Thank God Almighty,
We're free at last.

But the Emancipation Proclamation proved illusory.
Not a single slave gained immediate freedom.
It extended only to the States that had seceded from the Union.
It omitted loyal border states.
It exempted portions of the Confederacy already having fallen under
    Northern control.
Absent the North's military might and ultimate victory,
The Emancipation Proclamation would be but a dead letter.

Free at last.
Free at last.
Thank God Almighty,
We're free at last.

The North's expanding military victory kept black eyes on the freedom
    prize.
Black men joined the United States Army and Navy.
Having been liberated, they liberated others.
Tens of thousands of black Union soldiers and sailors,
Freed as they had been freed.
For some a war for federalism;
For them a war for freedom.

Free at last.
Free at last.
Thank God Almighty,
We're free at last.

But the word traveled slowly.
So slowly that it took years...
More than two-and-one-half years
For some of the liberated
To learn of their liberation.

Free at last.
Free at last.
Thank God Almighty,
We're free at last.

A latter day Paul Revere appeared in Galveston, Texas.
June 19, 1865.
Major General Gordon Granger delivered the news.
The Union triumphed over the rebellious Confederacy.
President Lincoln freed the slaves.

Free at last.
Free at last.
Thank God Almighty,
We're free at last.

The word spread.
West of the Mississippi.
Plantation to plantation.

Free at last.
Free at last.
Thank God Almighty,
We're free at last.

Whispers.
Shouts.
A hallelujah chorus.

Free at last.
Free at last.
Thank God Almighty,
We're free at last.

That day in June.
That fateful day.
June 19, 1865.
Freedom Day.
The day emancipation touched down.

"And upon this act, sincerely believed to be an act of justice, warranted
by the Constitution, upon military necessity, I invoke the considerate
judgment of mankind, and the gracious favor of Almighty God."
Abraham Lincoln, *President of the United States of America*

*Amazing Grace*
*Rosa Louise Parks*


A seamstress.
An ordinary woman.
A simple life.

Dignified in the face of indignity.
Loving in the face of hatred.
Hopeful in the face of despair.

Rosa Louise Parks.
Sister Rosa.
Mother of the modern civil rights movement.

A civil rights activist.
Active in voter registration.
Active in the defense of the Scottsboro Boys.
Active as NAACP branch secretary and youth advisor.

The segregated South.
Montgomery, Alabama.
Belly of the beast.

December 1, 1955.
A city bus.
"White" and "Colored" sections.
Black in the back.

Enter Rosa Parks.
Tired from working.
Tired of waiting.
Just plain tired.

A peevish driver.
A full white section.
A white man left standing.
A woman who would not be moved.

Rosa refused to relinquish her seat
Knowing full well the consequences.

Arrest.
Conviction.
A $10 fine; $4 in court fees.
The launch of a movement.
Not here.
Not now.
Not anymore.
Segregation must end!

Jo Ann Robinson planned a one-day bus boycott.
Students plastered the community with flyers.
Local ministers met.
They backed the boycott,
And announced it from their pulpits.

The bus boycott proved a resounding success.
The Montgomery Improvement Association emerged.
Martin Luther King, Jr. took the helm.
The boycott gained new momentum
And continued until December 21, 1956.

They walked.
They created a private jitney service.
They surreptitiously took rides from sympathetic whites.
They did what they had to do.

Bus ridership plummeted.
Bus company revenue dwindled.
Economic pressures proved too costly to bear.

Political chicanery.
Legal maneuvering.
Bombings.

White Montgomery,
Official Montgomery,
Tried it all.
But to no avail.

Blacks remained steadfast.
Blacks remained nonviolent.

Montgomery would never be the same.
And neither would the United States of America.
On November 13, 1956, the United States Supreme Court declared
   segregation on buses unconstitutional.

It all began on an ordinary day
With an ordinary woman
On an ordinary city bus.

Rosa Louise Parks.
Sister Rosa.
Mother of the modern civil rights movement.

A seamstress.
An ordinary woman.
A simple life.

Amazing.
Grace.
Her amazing grace.

We were blind,
But now we see.

We were lost,
But now we are found.

Rosa Louise Parks.
An eternal flame
In a world transformed.

Thank you, Rosa Parks.

Thank you for opening our eyes.
Thank you for showing us the way.
Thank you for lighting our path.

## Healing History

Unfortunate history,
Unpardonable sin,
Wretched deeds,
Where to begin?

Riots and lynchings,
And dastardly deeds,
Here in America,
Sowing the seeds.

Hate and violence,
Darkness and despair,
Moments in time,
Lacking in care.

Untold stories,
Of privation and pain,
Unheralded heroes,
Insoluble stain.

Lies and deceptions,
Some great, some small,
Diminish our standing,
Not one, but all.

Cuts and bruises,
Scrapes and scars,
Pages of history,
Legacy of wars.

Festering wounds,
Unhealed by time,
Regret and remembrance,
Of actors and crimes.

History remains,
Inconvenient, perhaps,
Our ignorance, though,
Sets its own traps.

Healing our history,
Knowing the truth,
Binds us together,
Elder and youth.

## Of Black & Jew

Viewed with suspicion.
Viewed with fear.

Scorned.
Excluded.
Ghettoized.

Prejudice.
Persecution.
Vilification.
Violence.

Pogrom.
Diaspora.
Holocaust.

Zionism,
A Zionist-inspired "Back-to-Africa" movement,
And countless black churches called Zion.
And spirituals—
We march upward to Zion;
We walk in Jerusalem.

The Black.
The Jew.

Common themes.
Common threads.
Parallel histories.

Shared suffering
The relativity of which
Seems relatively insignificant.

Paths diverging.
Paths crossing.
Paths diverging once more.

Suspicious.
Fearful.
Too often of one another.

Like amnesic strangers
Unaware of past lives
And those with whom they shared them.

We forget that blacks and Jews
Came together to fight bias and bigotry and to empower black
    communities
By creating the National Association for the Advancement of Colored
    People in 1909
And the National Urban League in 1910.

We forget Julius Rosenwald,
Jewish corporate executive,
Who built rural black schools and urban YMCAs.

We forget that Mr. Rosenwald
Used his wealth and influence
To bolster the fledgling school
Of his black brother, Booker T. Washington—
Tuskegee Institute.

We forget Joel Elias Spingarn,
Jewish educator and literary critic,
Who led the NAACP in its infancy.

We forget black newspapers
Who stood firmly against Nazism
Before the mainstream press.

We forget the thousands of Black soldiers,
Second-class citizens at home,
Who fought against Nazi oppression in World War II.

We forget that Jewish professors,
Refugees from World War II,
Found safe havens at black colleges in the South,
And began building black/white bridges
Based on empathy and shared experience.

We forget that Jews swelled the ranks of civil rights attorneys in the
1960s South
And worked within the system to change the system.
They did so, along with their black brothers and sisters, at great
sacrifice and personal peril.

We forget the organizations
Central to the struggle against racial prejudice—
The American Jewish Committee.
The American Jewish Congress.
The Anti-Defamation League.

We forget the young lives we lost in the struggle
Like Andrew Goodman and Michael Schwerner,
Young Jewish men.
Civil rights workers in the Deep South,
Martyred with James Chaney

For black liberation,
But as much for white liberation.
For the liberation of America.

We forget.
We all forget.
And we drift further and further apart.

Black nationalism.
Jewish assimilation.
Relative Jewish wealth
Juxtaposed against relative black privation.
Persistent white racism.
Affirmative action.
Louis Farrakhan.

So much intervening.
Fissures
Cracks in the foundation,
Yet not irreparably so.

Our common bonds,
Born of experiences and relationships,
Must not be allowed to come unloosened
Simply on account of neglect.

We must never forget.
The history we share
Is worth reclaiming.

*American Iconography*
*And the King I Know*

Baptist minister
Ph.D. in theology
Nobel Laureate
Civic leader
Activist
Provocateur
Raconteur
Orator extraordinaire
Freedom fighter
Peacemaker
Martyr

Inspired by Gandhi;
Mentored by Mays.

The Reverend Dr. Martin Luther King, Jr.—
The King I know.

The King I know:
Blessed with a faithful partner.
Coretta Scott—
The King's queen,
Sometimes a step or two behind him,
Sometimes in lockstep with him,
Occasionally a few steps ahead.

The King I know:
A man who moved people,
Inspired them to unimagined heights,
Touched them at unexplored depths.

The King I know:
A man who identified with
And became identified as
A movement—
An American movement.
A movement for black civil rights.
A movement to free the oppressed
And likewise to free their oppressors.

The King I know:
A man who grew and evolved,
And saw the need for systemic change.
A man who connected the dots
Of racism
And poverty
And materialism
And jingoism
And xenophobia
And colonialism
And militarism.

The King I know:
A man who dined with presidents and princes,
At home and abroad.
A man who lived with the poor in Chicago slums
And marched alongside sanitation workers in Memphis.

The King I know:
A man who rolled with the punches—
An assailant's knife.

Beatings.
Bombings.
FBI wiretaps.
Smear campaigns.
Organizational infighting.

The King I know:
A man who turned the other cheek,
And met violence with the full fury of nonviolent reaction.

The King I know:
A man obedient by nature
Who taught us civil disobedience.

The King I know:
A great man,
And, like all great men,
Fallible and flawed.

The King I know:
A man wise beyond his years
Who had been to the mountaintop,
Seen the Promised Land,
And will not get there with us.
Struck down by an assassin's bullet at thirty-nine.

His legacy—
A more perfect Union.
Less racism.
True citizenship for African-Americans.
More integration.
Opportunity more equally distributed.
Hope.

That's the King I know.

The King I know:
Honored with a national holiday—
And countless city streets
And public schools
And municipal parks
And commemorative parades
And celebrity tributes
And memorial services
From coast to coast
From border to border.

But this is America.
Land of shibboleth and symbol.
Short stories.
Sound bites.
Icons.

The King I know:
Seems one-dimensional in death.
Reduced to "I Have A Dream";
To bland recitations
Of powerful words
Without context to give them life—
And without works to give them breath.

We honor the King I know
In how we live
And move
And have our being.
When we become change agents—
Catalysts.
When we serve, selflessly,
For the greater good.

If we did that
The King I know
Would be proud.

## *Our Diversity Moments*

Potent and poignant.
Insightful and incisive.
Heart-rending and heart-warming.
These are our diversity moments:

I'm a black male. In high school, I told my principal that I wanted to attend college. He replied, "You'll be in state prison by the time you're 21."

I'm white. I thought of myself as a tolerant person. I was recently watching a television show with my eleven-year-old son. The show featured a black family. I told my son, "Isn't it amazing how articulate this black family is?" (I thought this was a positive comment.) My son replied, "Yes, Dad, but isn't it amazing that you're amazed?"

My favorite Christmas gift at age sixteen was a Johnny Mathis album, "Portrait of Johnny." My sister gave it to me and I was thrilled. When my father found out, he grabbed the album and threw it into the fireplace. I don't think that I ever forgave my racist father— ever!

I'm black. A white lady saw my little girl and asked to pick her up. Then she said, "She's one of the cleanest ones I've seen in a long time."

My husband's brother died of AIDS. He was gay. Because of family and religious pressure, he did not stay in a monogamous relationship. A week after his death and funeral, my husband and I were with our closest friends when they started to tell AIDS jokes. My husband was not able to tell them his brother was gay and had died of AIDS. I had to respect his wishes and remain quiet while our friends said things that hurt us both deeply.

Having been single all my adult life—single and unattached—I've had to deal with rumors about being a lesbian. I am not, but I find it interesting that so many others have decided that I must be because of my independence and friends. Often men make this judgment—I think simply because of my personal strength and lack of need for them.

I worked in an office where senior management was all male. They liked to "hug" female subordinates. I didn't participate. One day my boss, a female, called me into her office and told me that I needed to be "more friendly" to the senior management.

I was not hired for a position because I was a single parent with two children. The interviewer told me I should find a husband and stay home and take care of my children.

My boss said in response to my request for a raise, "You're married. Your husband makes lots of money."

My son's seventh grade basketball team was scheduled to play in their league's semifinal game on a Saturday morning. As luck would have it, there was also a Bar Mitzvah that morning and the whole team had been invited. The boys themselves voted to request that the game time be changed. The league refused to honor the request. The boys then all agreed to forfeit the game and attend the Bar Mitzvah.

When I was in middle school a boy in my class drew a cartoon depicting members of my religion tied up before a firing squad. He then folded it and passed it up to me. When I opened it, I was horrified. I realized that he was just trying to hurt me, and it worked. I'll never forget that drawing. It impressed upon me the intolerance that people can show.

I suffered an injury at age eighteen that left me paralyzed from the waist down and wheelchair bound. Following my injury, I went to an ice cream shop with my grandmother. The attendant looked at me, then she asked my grandmother what I wanted.

I was shopping with a wheelchair bound child. An older, well-dressed woman came up and asked, "How can you bring such a poor little thing out in public?"

Diversity moments.
Significant incidents that remind us that we are somehow different.

*Different on account of race.*
*Different on account of ethnicity.*
*Different on account of color.*
*Different on account of national origin.*
*Different on account of gender.*
*Different on account of religion.*
*Different on account of sexual orientation.*
*Different on account of age.*
*Different on account of economic status.*
*Different on account of ability status.*

Different.
Just different.

We value diversity when we listen to the stories of others.
An insensitive remark.
An unthinking action.
All on account of differences.

But different is different.
Not better.
Not worse.
Different.

Respect differences.
Uphold individual human dignity.
Honor our shared humanity.

These are our diversity moments.

## The Convert

If I could strip away my black skin,
And the way it makes me feel,
What would be the consequence?
Would my reality then be real?

If by simply wishing it,
I could become white,
What would that accomplish?
Would it give me new insight?

Would I somehow feel less burdened,
By the baggage dark skin brings?
Would I scale new mountain vistas?
Would I nest among the kings?

Would I recognize "my people,"
Though no longer of their ilk?
Or ignore the cloak of darkness,
Accustomed now to silk?

Though we've made much progress,
We've miles before we sleep.
And color makes some difference,
Still promises left to keep.

I know for sure this one thing:
We're different and the same.
What we have in common,

Goes by just one name.

Shared humanity links us,
In spite of what we do.
Appreciate the differences,
But let humanity shine through.

*Bridges*

Build us a bridge
Across oceans blue,
Over man-made chasms,
O'er hearts and minds, too.

Bridges that link,
Ties that bind,
Connections that comfort,
Make life so sublime.

Spanning life's seas,
Arching life's skies,
Joining the masses,
Answering cries.

Atypical engineering,
No concrete, no steel.
Mind over matter,
What we know; what we feel.

Bridges, not fences
Will set us all free,
Connections to others—
Those we don't see.

Join us in ways
We now only dream,
*E pluribus unum*,

Made more than a theme.

Build us a bridge
Across oceans blue,
Over man-made chasms,
O'er hearts and minds, too.

# Epilogue

As a young black child, immaturity and the lack of sufficient life experiences allowed me to minimize, if not wholly avoid, troubling questions of race. Adolescence and youth signaled the end of innocence.

Like a long-dormant volcano, such questions erupted into my consciousness with unanticipated ferocity. Like lava, my hyperconsciousness cooled, and then congealed, over time.

What makes someone who would like nothing better than to move beyond race—someone like me—come to the painful conclusion that race remains a crippling, chronic dynamic in our shared culture? Life. Living.

It is precisely the extraordinary ordinariness of racism—its institutionalization—that makes it so insidious and society so susceptible to its wiles. What, then, are we to do?

Without doubt, we live the legacy of a race-based system of privilege and pain. Yet, we cannot allow ourselves to become fixated on, obsessed with, or intoxicated by, it. To acknowledge the reality of racism and seek its eradication is not, perforce, to be consumed by it.

As we run against the winds of racism, we deflect it for those who follow. The running is swifter in our wake.

Through thoughtful and empathetic consideration of and appreciation for our differences—and, more fundamentally, our similarities—we may finally unite black and white, male and female, rich and poor, and beyond. We may produce a more tolerant, and, ultimately, more accepting, society.

Most of us want to take constructive advantage of our diversity and come together around our commonalities in service of a greater good. That must be the new American way.

# ABOUT THE AUTHOR

Hannibal B. Johnson is a graduate of Harvard Law School and The University of Arkansas. Johnson is an attorney, author, consultant, and college professor.

Active in community and civic affairs, Johnson is past president of Leadership Tulsa, past president of the Metropolitan Tulsa Urban League and past president of the Northeast Oklahoma Black Lawyers Association. He is the director of Anytown, Oklahoma, a statewide human relations/diversity camp for teens. Johnson has served as chairman of the board of directors of The Community Leadership Association, an international leadership organization, is a founding director of the Oklahoma Appleseed Center for Law and Justice, and serves on the board of directors of the Oklahoma Department of Libraries. Johnson is a member of the Oklahoma State University Center for Health Science College of Osteopathic Medicine Institutional Review Board. He serves on the Advisory Board of the Mayborn Literary Nonfiction Writers Conference of the Southwest.

Johnson's previous books include: *Black Wall Street—From Riot to Renaissance in Tulsa's Historic Greenwood District; Up From the Ashes—A Story About Community; Acres of Aspiration—The All-Black Towns in Oklahoma; Mama Used to Say—Wit & Wisdom From The Heart & Soul;* and *No Place Like Home—A Story About an All-Black, All-American Town.*

Johnson's honors include: the "Don Newby/Ben Hill" award from

Tulsa Metropolitan Ministry; the "Keeping The Dream Alive" award from the Dr. Martin Luther King, Jr. Commemoration Society; the "Outstanding Service to the Public Award" from the Oklahoma Bar Association; the "Ten Outstanding Young Tulsans" award from the Tulsa Jaycees; the "Distinguished Leadership Award" from the National Association for Community Leadership; the 2005 "Ralph Ellison Literary Award" from the Black Liberated Arts Center; the 2006 Oklahoma Human Rights Award from the Oklahoma Human Rights Commission; and induction into the 100 Black Men of Tulsa, Inc. "Hall of Honor" in 2007.

# WHAT PEOPLE ARE SAYING ABOUT
# INCOGNEGRO
*Poetic Reflections on Race & Diversity in America*

"The topic of race and diversity in America is too often relegated to references to the 'race card,' as though this serious topic is nothing more than a game. Such references...allow those who find it in their interest to avoid discussing and addressing race and diversity issues to belittle the real and tangible impact racial discrimination and bias continue to have in our society. This work is another opportunity to shed a light on these topics and will hopefully generate thoughtful dialogue and meaningful action."
 – **Albert E. Dotson, Jr., Esq.**, *Miami Attorney & President, 100 Black Men of America, Inc.*

"Hannibal Johnson can write 'Angry Black Man' but he is not one. Hannibal is a mature, sensitive, clear-eyed observer and bridge-builder. His sense of history's lessons—and he is always the wise student of human nature and experience—leads him to seek the firm middle ground rather than the extremes. Insights into the challenges, visions, and hopes for blacks and inspiration for people of every color, class, and creed fill these poignant and powerful poems. Comfortable in his own skin, Hannibal helps us appreciate our differences, while letting our shared humanity shine through."
 – **Rabbi Charles P. Sherman**, *Temple Israel, Tulsa, Oklahoma*

"*IncogNegro* helps us uncloak the kind of thinking, believing, and actions that continue to divide us as a nation, especially along racial lines. These reflections on race and diversity in America will touch your heart, your very soul, and make you want to—no, **make you**—holler, 'Stop the Madness!' It is time to start a new, more positive chapter in our history. *IncogNegro* helps us to do just that."

– **Dr. Cornell Thomas**, *Vice President, Institutional Diversity, Oklahoma State University*


"*IncogNegro* is a thought provoking poetic introduction to a discussion about race and diversity. It is a refreshing and enlightening read as a prelude to understanding race relations today."

– **Dr. Lonnie R. Williams**, *Associate Vice Chancellor, Division of Student Affairs, Arkansas State University*

CPSIA information can be obtained at www.ICGtesting.com
Printed in the USA
LVOW12s1111150615

442515LV00001B/150/P